# SCIENTISTS Get Dressed

By DEBORAH LEE ROSE

PERSNICKETY PRESS

Photos curated by Deborah Lee Rose
Designed by Shan Stumpf
Edited by Caroline Watkins

Library of Congress Cataloging-in-Publication
Data available.

ISBN: 978-1-943978-48-9

Printed in Canada at Friesens Corporation
cpsia tracking label information
Production Location: Altona, Manitoba
Production Date: 8/2/2019
Cohort: Batch No. 255072

10 9 8 7 6 5 4 3 2 1

PERSNICKETY
PRESS

Published by Persnickety Press
An imprint of WunderMill, Inc.
120A North Salem Street
Apex, NC 27502

For Sylvie and Sawyer,
and their mom and dad
who brave ice and wind
to do science and engineering

In memory of my colleague
and friend, Dr. Marian Diamond,
world renowned brain scientist
and brilliant teacher—who
wore a white lab coat when she
did research, and carried a
preserved human brain in a
hatbox when she went to teach

www.wundermillbooks.com

# SCIENTISTS
## Get Dressed

# From head

Mae Jemison's astronaut helmet and spacesuit must fit and work perfectly. They're designed to protect her during blastoff and return to Earth on the space shuttle. All astronauts get help "donning" (putting on) and checking their suits and helmets for their space missions.

Astronauts' spacesuits and gear supply them with oxygen and drinking water, let them communicate, and keep them warm or cool enough. As technology advances, spacesuit design also changes to make new kinds of space work and space travel possible.

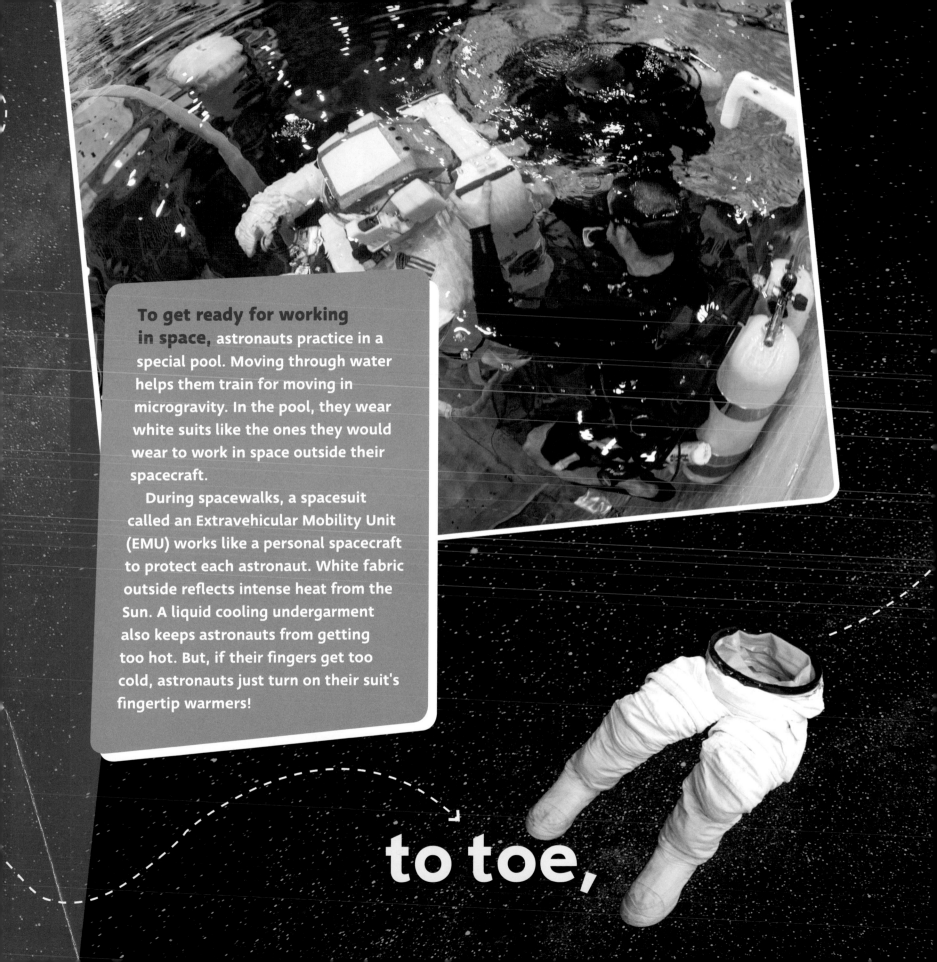

To get ready for working in space, astronauts practice in a special pool. Moving through water helps them train for moving in microgravity. In the pool, they wear white suits like the ones they would wear to work in space outside their spacecraft.

During spacewalks, a spacesuit called an Extravehicular Mobility Unit (EMU) works like a personal spacecraft to protect each astronaut. White fabric outside reflects intense heat from the Sun. A liquid cooling undergarment also keeps astronauts from getting too hot. But, if their fingers get too cold, astronauts just turn on their suit's fingertip warmers!

to toe,

**Marian Diamond puts on her white lab coat to study the brain** and how it changes as it grows. She finds that enriching our brains—with new challenges, fun, and even love—can make our brains work better, from when we are very young to when we are old. And when she teaches about the brain, she brings a preserved human brain to class in a hatbox!

Many kinds of scientists wear lab coats, and if needed, they add gloves, masks, and goggles. These help protect scientists from germs or chemicals, and keep scientists' own germs from coming in contact with what the scientists are handling.

# scientists get dressed for the work they do

**Melanie Hayden Gephart puts on a mask, hat, magnifying glasses, sterile gown, and gloves** to do brain surgery in an operating room. Before she gowns up, she washes her hands and arms extremely well. All surgeons take these steps to protect their patients from germs during surgery.

Her gloves are very flexible, so she can hold her surgical tools tightly and move them carefully. The glasses she wears let her see tiny parts of the brain, like nerves and blood vessels, when she operates to remove brain tumors.

# and the places they do it!

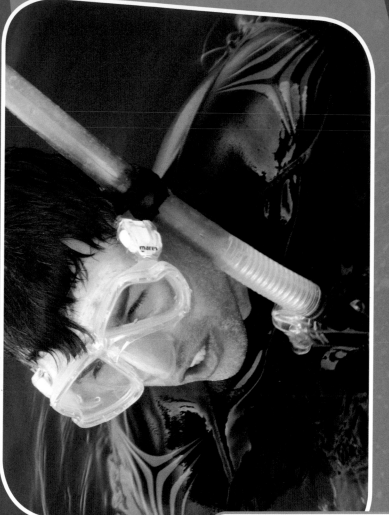

Eric Hoffmayer swims with the biggest fish in the ocean—endangered whale sharks. As large as school buses, these giants swim fast, even when they barely move their tails. He wears his mask, snorkel, and swim fins to help him follow whale sharks near the ocean surface, seeing as many as 100 feeding together!

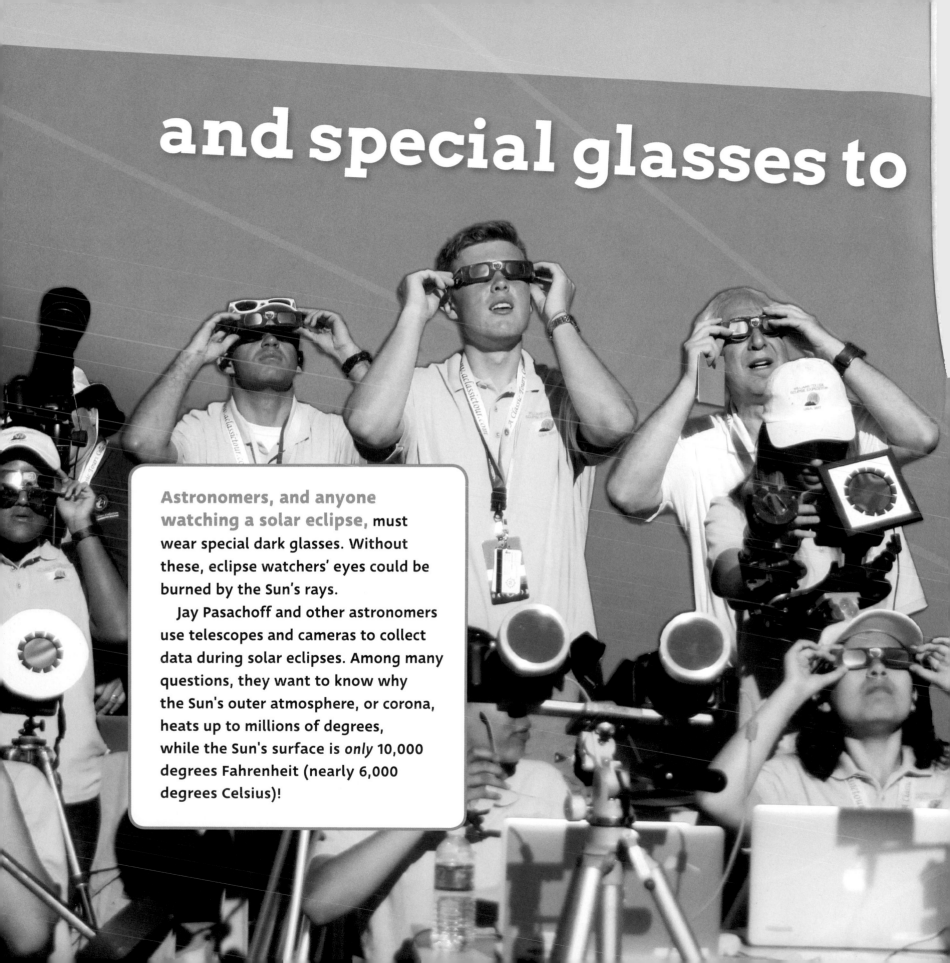

# and special glasses to

Astronomers, and anyone watching a solar eclipse, must wear special dark glasses. Without these, eclipse watchers' eyes could be burned by the Sun's rays.

Jay Pasachoff and other astronomers use telescopes and cameras to collect data during solar eclipses. Among many questions, they want to know why the Sun's outer atmosphere, or corona, heats up to millions of degrees, while the Sun's surface is *only* 10,000 degrees Fahrenheit (nearly 6,000 degrees Celsius)!

When bats make their night flights, scientists can use night vision goggles to watch them. Bats "see" in the dark using echolocation. This little brown bat is finding its prey by sending out sound waves and listening to the echoes that bounce off other animals and objects. Echolocation helps bats hunt without bumping into each other!

Some caves are roosts for about 20,000 to 50,000 endangered Indiana bats! Especially when so many gather together, keeping wild bats healthy is important. Certain species eat billions of insects that could make humans sick and damage trees or crops. Other bat species pollinate plants that grow different foods people eat around the world, like bananas, mangoes, and chocolate.

# Scientists wear helmets and headlamps to count bats in dark caves,

**Bill Moore counts bats hibernating in winter caves** and checks bats for disease. He wears his own light on his protective helmet. Scientists must clean their clothing and gear after each cave visit, to help prevent spreading disease and microscopic organisms from one bat colony to another.

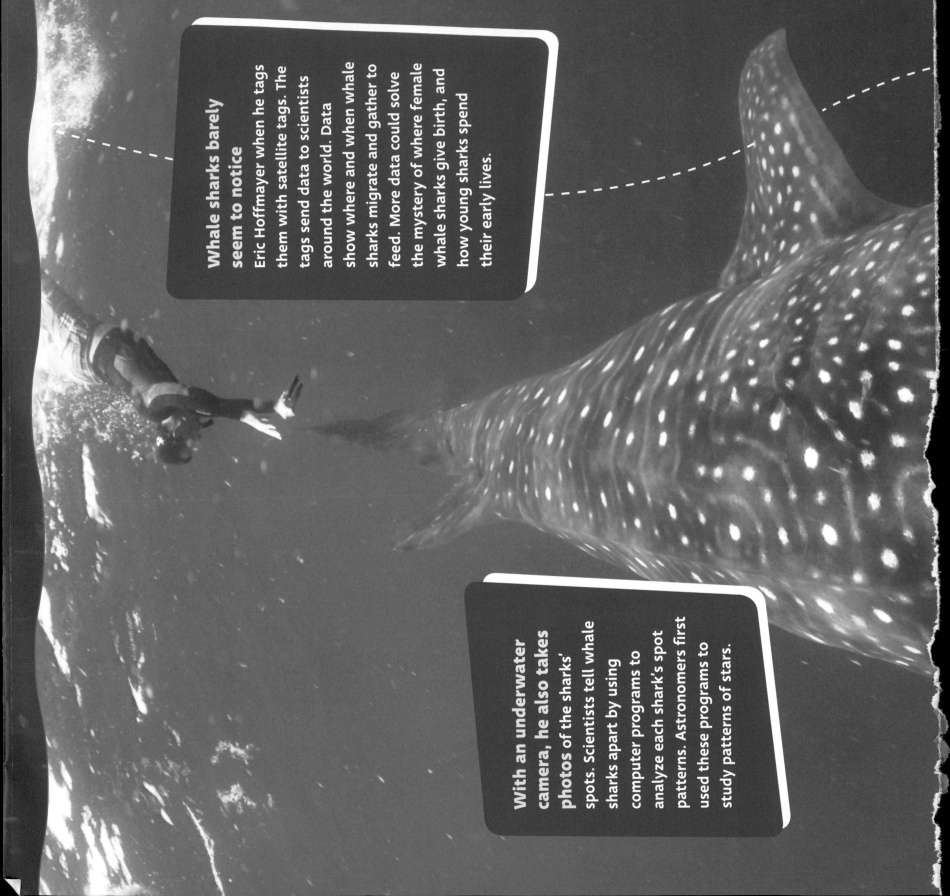

**Whale sharks barely seem to notice**
Eric Hoffmayer when he tags them with satellite tags. The tags send data to scientists around the world. Data show where and when whale sharks migrate and gather to feed. More data could solve the mystery of where female whale sharks give birth, and how young sharks spend their early lives.

**With an underwater camera, he also takes photos of the sharks'** spots. Scientists tell whale sharks apart by using computer programs to analyze each shark's spot patterns. Astronomers first used these programs to study patterns of stars.

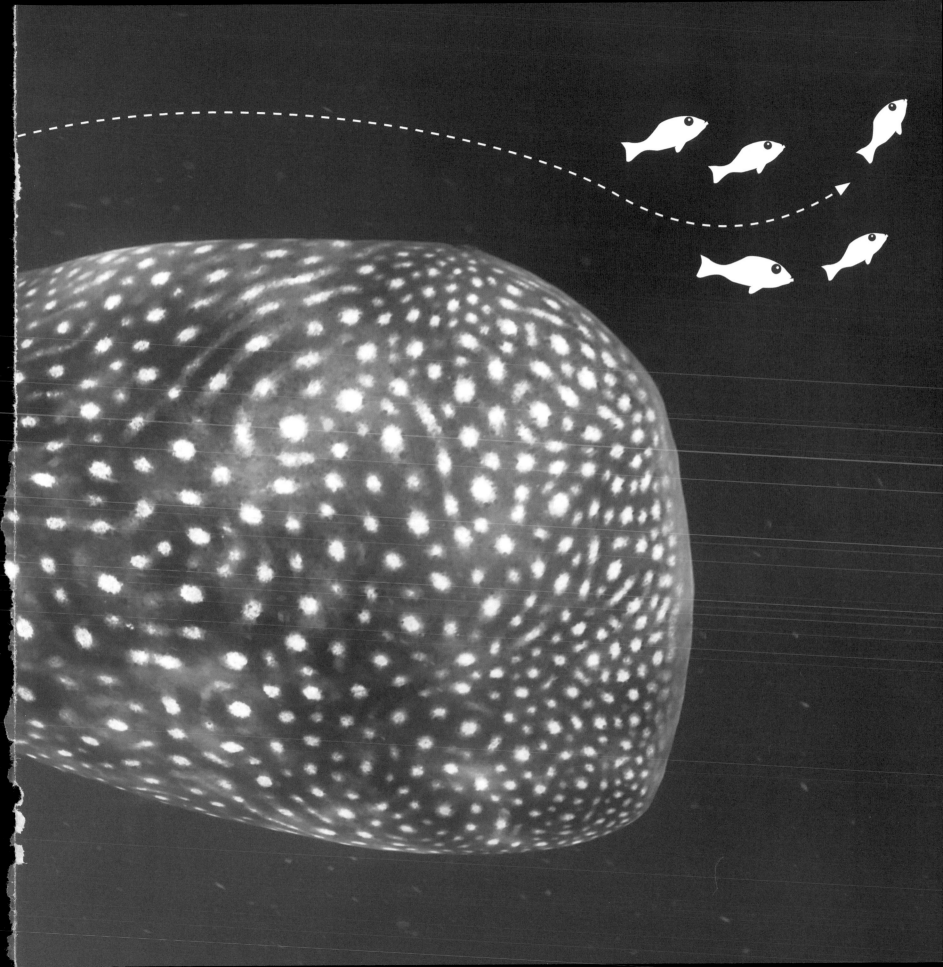

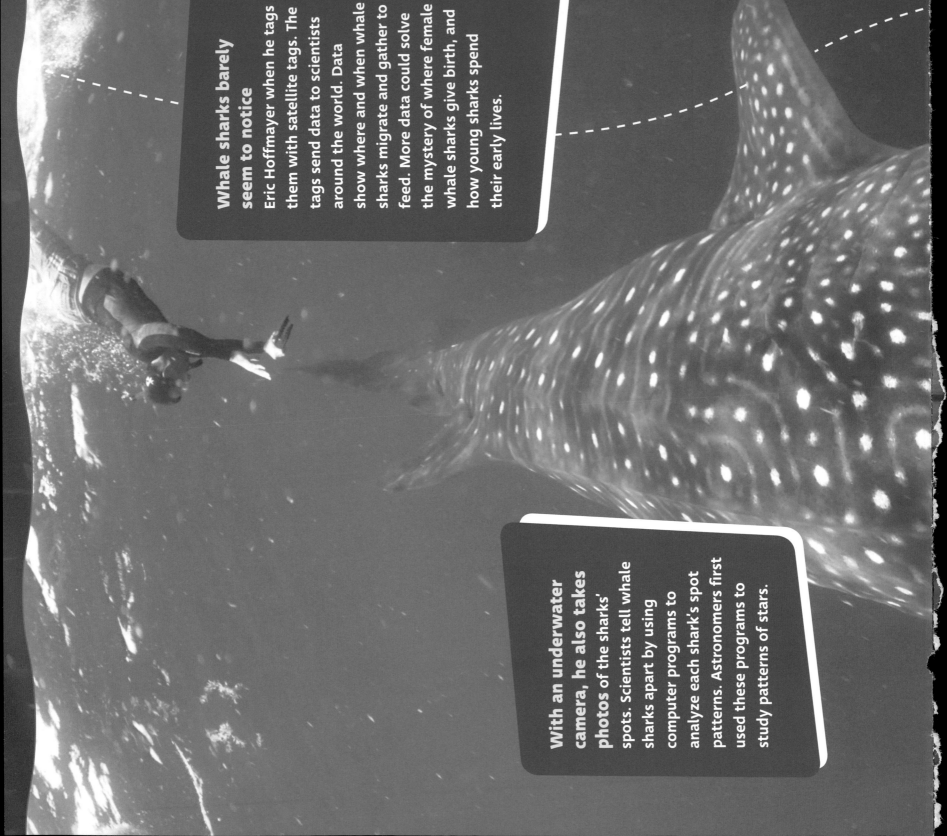

**Whale sharks barely seem to notice**
Eric Hoffmayer when he tags them with satellite tags. The tags send data to scientists around the world. Data show where and when whale sharks migrate and gather to feed. More data could solve the mystery of where female whale sharks give birth, and how young sharks spend their early lives.

**With an underwater camera, he also takes photos of the sharks' spots.** Scientists tell whale sharks apart by using computer programs to analyze each shark's spot patterns. Astronomers first used these programs to study patterns of stars.

# watch the Sun during a solar eclipse.

The best time to see and study the Sun's superhot corona is during an eclipse's "totality." This is the phase when the Moon moves completely in front of the Sun. For a very short time, the two spheres seem the same size. The Sun is really about 400 times bigger than the Moon, but the illusion happens because the Sun is also 400 times farther away from us than the Moon is from Earth.

# Scientists wear harnesses to climb high up in the forest,

**Rebecca Tripp gets into a climbing harness,** then hooks the harness to pull ropes that let her reach the forest canopy. By using harnesses and ropes, scientists can get close enough to study animals living in and visiting this highest part of the forest. Gloves guard her hands from rope burn.

Tardigrade

These eight-legged, microscopic organisms known as "water bears" are found in water and damp places everywhere on Earth. They can survive many years without water or food, and even stay alive in the extreme conditions of space!

When she comes down from the canopy, she brings forest samples she collected. Back in the lab, she examines them under a microscope. She studies extremely tiny creatures called "water bears" or tardigrades.

**Bob Thirsk skydives from a plane** for astronaut training. When the parachute he's wearing opens in midair, it slows him down for a safe landing on the ground or on water. Astronauts also train for how they would use their parachutes for shelter or protective clothing. This could be needed if, on return to Earth, they landed in a remote area or extreme environment.

# and parachutes to skydive down through the clouds.

Our brain and senses help us know up from down—like whether we're standing up or doing a handstand. In the microgravity of space, astronauts may find this more difficult, and could make mistakes as a result. In the International Space Station, Bob Thirsk helps study how astronauts perceive up and down.

To practice for space, astronauts also ride in a special airplane where they can be weightless. The plane's steep up and down flight pattern lets astronauts (and others) experience weightlessness multiple times during each flight. For 20-30 seconds at a time, passengers can float, flip, and feel what moving in space is like.

# On a volcano, they pull on thick gloves to collect burning lava.

**Jessica Ball wears thick cotton gloves** and cotton clothing that won't rip easily or melt near hot lava. Gloves help shield her face from lava's burning heat and protect her hands from sharp volcanic rock and glass. Lava samples give scientists clues to what's happening deep under Earth's surface. This could help scientists better predict eruptions and save people's lives and property.

When a volcano spews lava high and far, Jessica Ball needs her safety helmet to protect her head. The respirator covering her nose and mouth filters out toxic sulfur gas so she can breathe safely.

In a helicopter, she wears a flight safety helmet while watching a full eruption from high above.

Adrian McCallum needs a parka, face mask, gloves, snow pants, thermal underclothing, boots, and crampons to work in the coldest, snowiest, iciest places on Earth. In the morning, in places like the Arctic and Antarctica, his outer expedition clothing feels like a frozen suit of armor until it thaws out.

Studying ice and snow helps Adrian McCallum learn how these forms of water freeze, melt, and travel down mountains as slow-moving glaciers and roaring avalanches.

Scientists' work to provide avalanche warnings could save the lives of mountain climbers and people living on snow-covered mountains around the world. Scientists' studies of how climate change is affecting Earth's polar caps, sea ice, and the coldest parts of the ocean could help save the planet.

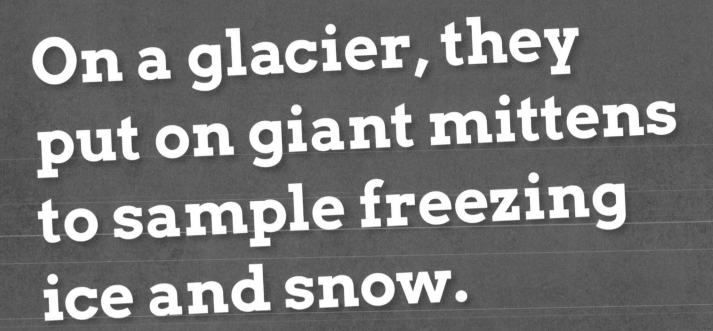

# On a glacier, they put on giant mittens to sample freezing ice and snow.

**To keep his hands from freezing,** he sometimes wears four pairs of mittens at the same time! So many mittens make it more difficult to handle tools for collecting snow and ice samples.

Scientists study sea turtles and their young in the ocean and on nesting beaches. Measuring and weighing turtles gives Meg Lamont data to help their survival.

Meg Lamont wears waterproof boots to rescue sea turtles. When warm ocean water gets too cold, turtles' metabolism slows way down. Then they have little energy to swim or lift their heads above water to breathe. To try and save cold-stunned turtles' lives, scientists gather as many as they can from the ocean, beaches, and marshes.

# They wear boots to get muddy when they rescue sea turtles,

Turtles are released into the ocean when the water warms up again. In the sea, turtles migrate long distances to lay their eggs on sandy beaches.

# and "bunny suits" to stay clean when they test equipment for space.

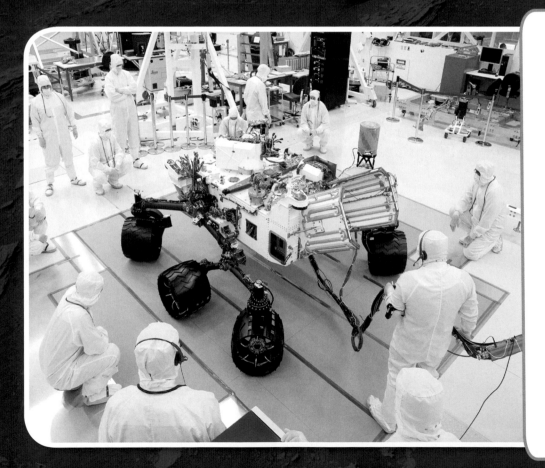

Space scientists and engineers put on head covers, masks, body suits, gloves, and booties to work in "clean rooms." They cover everything but their eyes. These coverings help keep dirt, dust, hair, and skin particles from ruining sensitive machines designed to work in space.

Special air filters, monitors, and lots of cleaning reduce the number of germs from Earth that could be carried on equipment, like a robotic rover, to Mars or other places far out in space.

The Mars robotic rover, Curiosity, explores the red planet's rocks, soil, and climate. Curiosity's overlapping photos, when pieced together, show huge views that are changing the scientific understanding of the Mars surface. Curiosity's analysis of Martian dirt found that water was present in soil—a major discovery.

# To dig dinosaur bones out of rock, scientists wear hiking boots and knee pads.

**Matt Wedel wears boots to climb and pads to protect his knees** when he hunts for fossils in dry, rocky places. He digs up dinosaur bones to learn how different life was on Earth millions of years ago. Removing bones from rock that surrounds them isn't easy. Sometimes a giant rock—with bones still in it—must be carried out by truck or lifted out by helicopter. Then the rock is taken to the lab, where scientists can carefully extract and study the ancient fossils.

Matt Wedel's field backpack holds his knee pads, rock hammer, shovel, water, toilet paper for wrapping fragile fossils, waterproof pens, and his notebook to make sketches of what he sees.

A model of an enormous, plant-eating sauropod's thigh bone is light enough to lift. A real dinosaur thigh bone, or femur, this size could weigh 10 times more. While some dinosaur backbones were filled with air, like modern bird bones, dinosaur legbones had thick walls and contained almost no air.

Matt Wedel's field backpack holds his knee pads, rock hammer, shovel, water, toilet paper for wrapping fragile fossils, waterproof pens, and his notebook to make sketches of what he sees.

Lucy Rose wears long, waterproof gloves and waders to work in streams, in all kinds of weather. For the coldest months, she may need hand warmers in her gloves and feet warmers in her waders.

In winter, she smashes through ice with a sledgehammer to reach moving water. She collects water to investigate how rain, plants, soil, and pollution change the stream from season to season. How fast the water moves at different times of year, and how much soil or pollution the water carries, affect things like the health of fish, other wildlife, and forests. Seasonal changes to streams can also affect the water we drink.

To study freshwater in streams, they wear waterproof gloves and waders.

In winter, frozen waders stand up by themselves!

# Where bees can sting, scientists need beekeepers' veils and suits.

Scott McArt wears his beekeeper's jacket and mesh veil when he studies live honey bees. He finds that when honey bees bring pollen back to the hive, they accidentally bring human-made chemicals too. Sometimes these chemicals, which are used to kill crop-eating insects or fungi, can end up killing many bees or harming them by changing their behavior.

One of the foods that "nurse" honey bees feed to baby bees, or larvae, is royal jelly. The jelly comes from glands in a nurse bee's head. To feed a bee larva, a nurse bee sticks her head into the larva's open cell and spits jelly into the cell. The larva eats the jelly while swimming in it!

Bees like this mining bee are critical to life on Earth. Around the world, many kinds of bee species pollinate plants that grow fruits, vegetables, and nuts people eat to survive. Understanding and protecting bee colonies doesn't just help bees, but humans too.

Full arm length gloves lined with Kevlar, which is stronger and lighter than steel, let Janie Veltkamp safely carry Beauty the Bald Eagle. Beauty got a 3D-printed, prosthetic beak after her real beak was shot off by a poacher.

A short falconer's glove, or gauntlet, lets a Peregrine Falcon perch safely and fly from Janie Veltkamp's wrist. Peregrine Falcons are the fastest birds in the world and can fly up to 200 miles (320 km) per hour.

# Where raptors can rip, scientists must have gloves and jackets that won't tear.

Janie Veltkamp's thick, leather jacket protects her arms, chest, and neck from a Bald Eagle's sharp beak and talons. She gloves her hands depending on how she's handling a bird of prey. Her protective clothing helps her rescue and care for sick and injured raptors like eagles, falcons, hawks, and owls, and release them back into the wild.

# Where raptors can rip, scientists must have gloves and jackets that won't tear.

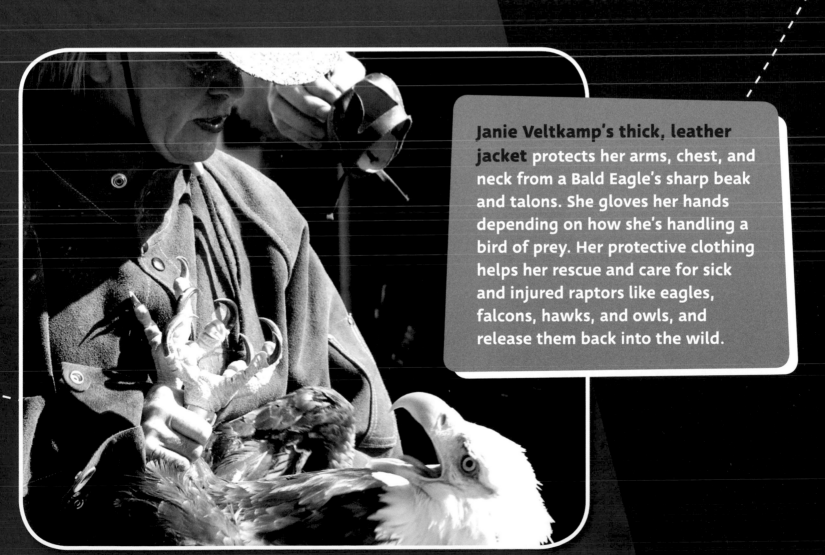

**Janie Veltkamp's thick, leather jacket** protects her arms, chest, and neck from a Bald Eagle's sharp beak and talons. She gloves her hands depending on how she's handling a bird of prey. Her protective clothing helps her rescue and care for sick and injured raptors like eagles, falcons, hawks, and owls, and release them back into the wild.

# Some scientists wear camouflage so wildlife won't know humans are nearby.

Tom Koerner camouflages himself to study and photograph different animals. The "ghillie suit" he wears over his clothing makes him look like sagebrush that grows on high mountain plains. When the ground is snowy, he switches to wearing a white poncho and white pants.

By blending in, he can get closer to animals like pronghorns, Snowy Owls, and coyotes. Watching wildlife closely lets scientists learn more about species' natural behaviors, and any threats to those species' survival.

# Other scientists wear costumes to look just like

Scientists who work with panda cubs wear full giant panda suits, purposely made to smell like panda poop and pee. They dress this way so young pandas won't know humans are taking care of them, and won't grow up dependent on humans for help later.

When cubs are old enough, they're moved to a partly wild habitat. They learn how to survive there on their own, before they can successfully live in the wild.

# the animals they help— even when it's not Halloween!

**Wild giant pandas are very rare,** and are found only in certain mountain areas of China. In the wild, panda cubs must quickly learn to climb trees to escape from predators like snow leopards. As adults, these bears spend most of their time looking for and eating bamboo shoots and leaves, which are almost the only food they eat.

# Photos Tell Science Stories

*Scientists Get Dressed* was inspired by the photo of a water scientist's frozen waders. Look closely at each photo in the book to answer these questions.

1. What is the scientist wearing?

2. What work is the scientist doing?

3. What tools or technology is the scientist using, and how?

4. Where is the scientist working?

5. What season or time of day was the photo taken?

6. Why do you think the scientist is dressed this way?

7. What might happen if the scientist wore different clothing?

8. Why do you think the scientist's work is important?

9. Do you have clothing or gear like any scientist in the book?

10. What do you do—or would you do—when wearing this clothing?

# Tell your own STEM stories

You can tell stories about STEM (science, technology, engineering, math) with photos. Use a camera, phone, or tablet device to take photos of scientists, animals, plants, rocks, snow, gear, technology, or anything in STEM that you want to know more about. You can talk about your photos—to your classmates, family, friends, or other people—just like real scientists do. Write about your photos, and you can make your own book!

# IF YOU WERE A SCIENTIST, HOW WOULD YOU GET DRESSED?

On my head I would wear _____

On my eyes I would wear _____

On my hands I would wear _____

On my feet I would wear _____

On my arms I would wear _____

On my legs I would wear _____

On my whole body I would wear _____

My favorite thing to wear would be _____

**Without the right size spacesuit,** an astonaut cannot safely perform a spacewalk. Peggy Whitson's suit, or extravehicular mobility unit (EMU), keeps her alive while working outside the International Space Station. She can read repair instructions in a booklet on her sleeve.

Scientists and engineers are improving spacesuit materials, technology, and design to make the suits more flexible, better fitting for different size astronauts, and adaptable for future space travel. How would you design a new spacesuit for a mission to the Moon or other planets?

Scientists do all kinds of work, with many different job names that tell what they do. As new specialties in science are created, so are new job titles. A scientist can have more than one kind of scientific job or specialty, and some scientists are also engineers. Mae Jemison is a doctor, chemical engineer, and astronaut. Adrian McCallum is a glaciologist, polar engineer, and oceanographer. Here are just some of the job titles of the scientists in *Scientists Get Dressed*.

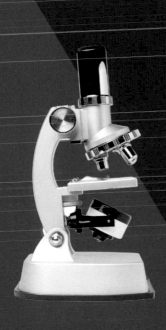

| | |
|---|---|
| Mae Jemison | doctor, chemical engineer, astronaut |
| Marian Diamond | neuroanatomist |
| Melanie Hayden Gephart | neurosurgeon |
| Eric Hoffmayer | marine biologist |
| Bill Moore | ecologist |
| Jay Pasachoff | astronomer |
| Rebeccca Tripp | forest canopy biologist |
| Bob Thirsk | doctor, astronaut |
| Jessica Ball | volcanologist |
| Adrian McCallum | glaciologist, polar engineer, oceanographer |
| Meg Lamont | biologist |
| Rover Team | space scientists and engineers |
| Matt Wedel | paleontologist |
| Lucy Rose | water chemist |
| Scott McArt | entomologist |
| Janie Veltkamp | raptor biologist |
| Tom Koerner | wildlife refuge manager |
| Panda scientists | conservation biologists |
| Peggy Whitson | biochemist, astronaut |

The Cornell Lab of Ornithology

# YOU CAN BE A CITIZEN SCIENTIST!

## WHAT IS CITIZEN SCIENCE?

Citizen science enables volunteers to help make scientific discoveries. There are many ways to help, such as making observations or recording information needed for scientific studies. Sometimes, citizen scientists even make their own scientific discoveries!

## HOW CITIZEN SCIENCE CAN CHANGE YOUR WORLD

### DISCOVER A NEW GALAXY!

Humans are sometimes better than computers at recognizing images. Many crowd-sourced science projects post photos online and ask volunteers to look for things in the images. Radio Galaxy Zoo (started by two Australian scientists) sends out telescope images of distant galaxies and asks people to tell scientists what they see. You can learn a lot about a galaxy by its shape, such as how old it might be, and whether it once collided with another galaxy.

Two Russian citizen scientists, Ivan Terentev and Tim Matorny, were comparing images and noticed something unusual. They reported it to scientists and were told that they had discovered a "wide-angle tail galaxy," a cluster of at least 40 galaxies. When it was published in a scientific paper, their discovery rocked the world of astronomers and physicists who said it was like finding a needle in a haystack. This galaxy, located more than one billion light-years from Earth, is now called the Matorny-Terentev Cluster.

Kids can gather scientific data at creeks and streams, with help and supervision from teachers, parents, or community leaders. Scientists can use data that kids gather about freshwater quality to protect frog and fish species, and other animals (including humans) that depend on healthy watersheds.

## HELP PROTECT BIRDS!

Tricolored Blackbirds live in colonies that move every year, which makes it hard for scientists to find and count them. In 2004, scientists tried to get this bird added to the California Endangered Species List but were unsuccessful. They knew the birds were declining in number, but they didn't have enough evidence to show it. Enter eBird, a project from the Cornell Lab of Ornithology that receives more than 100 million observations from citizen scientists every year.

In 2015, Tricolored Blackbirds were under consideration for protection again. Using data from eBird, ecologist Orin Robinson showed how the birds had declined by one-third over the previous ten years. Thanks to the observations of citizen scientists, the Tricolored Blackbird is now listed as a protected species in California.

## CAN I BE A CITIZEN SCIENTIST?

YES! Children of all ages have counted animals, taken cloud photos, recorded natural sounds, searched for stars with cell phones, and counted and identified birds for projects all over the world.

Celebrate Urban Birds brings outstanding youth, from communities that are not represented in the sciences, on full scholarships to attend workshops about birding, careers, conservation, and the arts at the Cornell Lab of Ornithology. Learn more at celebrateurbanbirds.org

# WHERE DO I START?

There are many different citizen-science projects you can participate in, wherever you live. Some of these projects are available as apps so you can do science even while you are waiting for the dentist. Other projects might bring you outdoors. There is something for everyone! A great place to start is SciStarter.org, where you can search for projects by what interests you—from frogs and butterflies, to air quality and earthquakes.

If you want to connect with birds and science, check out the Cornell Lab of Ornithology. Track and share your bird sightings anywhere, anytime with eBird or watch and record birds at your feeder for Project FeederWatch. In urban and suburban areas, you can get involved with community activities with Celebrate Urban Birds, or you can learn how to find and monitor bird nests in your neighborhood with NestWatch. Learn more about these projects at Birds.Cornell.edu/CitizenScience. You can get the whole family involved, or maybe just you. Who knows what you might discover?

# SCIENTISTS' GLOVE CHALLENGE

## WHAT KINDS OF GLOVES DO SCIENTISTS WEAR? ALL KINDS!

- Giant mittens to keep warm, for working on glaciers

- Gloves lined with Kevlar, stronger than steel, for handling rescued raptors

- Spacesuit gloves with fingertip warmers, for working outside a spacecraft

- Cotton gloves that won't melt, for working on volcanoes

- Waterproof gloves to keep dry and warm, for working in streams and lakes

- Tight-fitting, thin gloves that flex like a bare hand, for working in labs or operating rooms

## WHY DO SCIENTISTS WEAR DIFFERENT KINDS OF GLOVES?

- To protect their hands from freezing or burning

- To prevent their hands from getting cut, scraped, or exposed to germs or chemicals

- To keep their hands warm or cool

- To keep germs or dirt on their hands from reaching patients, lab samples, or sensitive pieces of equipment

## ACTIVITY THEME AND PURPOSE

Scientists can't do their work without the right clothing or tools—including gloves. Some gloves make scientific work more challenging. In this activity, learners try different tasks while wearing gloves that represent scientists' gloves. Learners begin to understand scientists' real, hands-on challenges. If you were a scientist, what gloves would you wear?

## WHAT YOU NEED
Depending on what is on hand or easily available, this activity can be done with various inexpensive types of gloves, and other inexpensive "tools" to test gloves in different tasks.

### POSSIBLE GLOVE TYPES
- Cotton work or garden gloves to represent a volcanologist's gloves
- Disposable, thin nitrile or other nonlatex gloves (any color) to represent a lab scientist's or neurosurgeon's gloves
- Thicker, ski-type gloves to represent an astronaut's space gloves
- Large mittens or oven mitts to represent a glaciologist's gloves
- Long, waterproof dishwashing gloves to represent a water scientist's gloves
- Noncotton work gloves to represent a paleontologist's gloves

### POSSIBLE TOOLS
- Tongs to pick things up
- Twist top water bottles (empty)
- Small sponges
- Measuring tape
- Washable markers and paper
- Lidded storage container
- Connectable toy bricks
- Optional: ice cubes in water

### WHAT TO DO
Try on each pair of gloves, to:
- Connect or build with toy bricks
- Open and close a lidded container
- Twist a water bottle top off and on
- Pick up objects with tongs
- Measure an object big or small
- Write with a marker

If you have ice cubes and water, test thin lab gloves vs. waterproof dish gloves by putting your gloved hands briefly in the icy water, to see which gloves keep your hands warmer.

### WHAT HAPPENED?
- Which gloves worked best with which tools and tasks?
- How do you think scientists decide which gloves to wear?
- Tell others, write down, or video your observations.

microgravity

volcano

talons

# Words

- 3D-printed
- astronaut
- astronomer
- atmosphere
- avalanche
- biologist
- blood vessels
- camouflage
- chemicals
- chemist
- citizen scientist
- clean room
- climate change
- collision
- computer program
- conservation
- corona
- crampons
- data
- donning
- echolocation
- eclipse

- ecologist
- ecosystem
- endangered
- engineer
- enriching
- entomologist
- environment
- eruption
- estimate
- expedition
- extravehicular mobility unit (EMU)
- femur
- filters
- forest canopy
- fossil
- fungi
- galaxy
- ghillie suit
- glacier
- glaciologist
- habitat

- harness
- hibernating
- illusion
- International Space Station
- investigate
- irruption
- Kevlar
- larva
- lava
- light-years
- magnifying
- marine biologist
- metabolism
- microgravity
- microscopic
- migration
- monitors
- nerves
- neuroanatomist
- neurosurgeon
- operating room
- organisms

- paleontologist
- parachute
- physicist
- polar
- pollinate
- pollution
- predator
- preserved
- prosthetic
- raptor
- respirator
- robotic rover
- satellite tag
- sauropod
- scientist
- SCUBA
- skydive
- sledgehammer
- snorkel
- sound waves
- space shuttle
- spacesuit
- spacewalk

- species
- sterile
- surgery
- survival
- talons
- tardigrade
- technology
- telescope
- totality
- toxic
- tumors
- volcano
- volcanologist
- waders
- weightlessness
- wildlife refuge

microscopic

# Q&A with Eric Hoffmayer

## Marine biologist and shark expert on educational poster

### Are whale sharks whales or sharks?

Whale sharks are sharks, not whales. They're named whale sharks due to their large size, but they have the anatomy of a shark, not a whale. For example, a whale shark has gills, rather than a blowhole, to breathe. Scientists mathematically estimate there are 119,000-238,000 whale sharks around the world.

### Why don't you wear SCUBA air tanks to swim with whale sharks?

It's mainly a safety concern. Whale sharks can dive from the surface to deeper water relatively quickly. If we wore SCUBA tanks and lost track of our depth while we were working, we could find ourselves in a dangerous situation. While we are conducting our research, we wear masks and snorkels to swim with whale sharks near the surface only.

### How does a satellite tag work?

Satellite tags record the location of the whale shark when it's at the surface. The battery-powered tags send data to scientists around the world. Typically, a tag comes off a whale shark's body within six months. Scientists are actively working on better attachments to collect data for a longer time.

### What can I do to help whale sharks?

The three biggest threats to whale sharks are collisions with ships, plastics in the ocean that get into their digestive system, and loss of habitat. To reduce the amount of plastic that ends up in the ocean, you can help by using fewer plastics, recycling plastics, and participating in beach cleanups and other events that positively impact the environment.

# NEXT GENERATION SCIENCE STANDARDS (NGSS) HIGHLIGHTS

## Science is a human endeavor:

Men and women from all cultures and backgrounds choose careers as scientists and engineers. Science affects everyday life. Creativity and imagination are important to science.

## Scientific investigations use a variety of methods:

Scientists use different ways to study the world. Science investigations use a variety of methods, tools, and techniques.

## Science knowledge is based on empirical evidence:

Science uses tools and technologies to make accurate measurements and observations.

## Science is a way of knowing:

Science knowledge helps us know about the world. Science is both a body of knowledge and the processes and practices used to add to that body of knowledge.

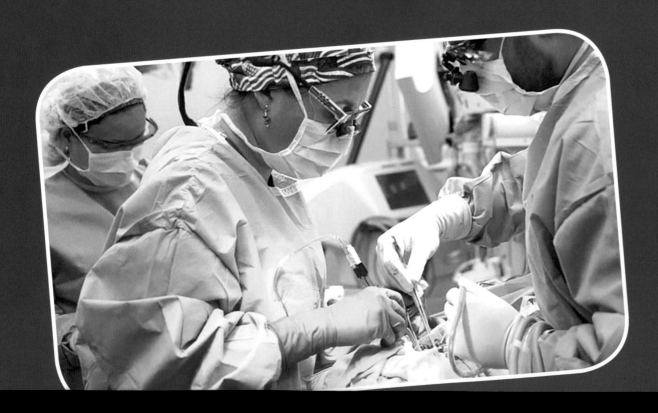

## Deborah Lee Rose

is the internationally published, award-winning author of *Scientists Get Dressed* and *Beauty and the Beak: How Science, Technology, and a 3D-Printed Beak Rescued a Bald Eagle*, both published by Persnickety Press. *Beauty and the Beak*, coauthored with Janie Veltkamp, has won the AAAS/Subaru SB&F Prize for Excellence in Science Books, the Bank Street College Cook Prize for Best STEM Picture Book, and the Eureka! Gold Award for Nonfiction. Her books include such beloved titles as *The Twelve Days of Kindergarten*, *The Twelve Days of Winter*, *Into the A, B, Sea* and *The People Who Hugged the Trees*. Deborah helped create the ALA/AASL honored, NSF-funded STEM education website howtosmile.org, and was senior science writer for UC Berkeley's renowned Lawrence Hall of Science. She graduated from Cornell University and lives in the Washington, DC area.

## Acknowledgments

So many people provided inspiration, images, and support for *Scientists Get Dressed*.

Extra thanks to Jessica Ball, The Berkshire Eagle, Ken Bogen, Miranda Bogen, Bonner County Daily Bee, Mia Cichetti, the Cornell Lab of Ornithology, Cornell University, Marian Diamond, Sylvia Earle, Melanie Hayden Gephart, Catherine Halversen, Martin Hartley, Eric Hoffmayer, Todd Holland, Glen Hush, Liat Kobza, Shelley Koerner, Tom Koerner, Lawrence Hall of Science, Meg Lowman, Scott McArt, Adrian McCallum, William Miller, Emma Mullen, Andy Murch, NASA, NOAA, Ethan Pawlowski, Matthew Rogerson, Lucy Rose, Sylvie Rose, Christine Royce, Robert Sanders, Anne Scanlon, Susan Schulman, Brian Scott Sockin, Steve Thomas, Rebecca Tripp, USFWS, USGS, Jane Veltkamp, and Mathew Wedel.

# Photo credits and permissions

WunderMill
CHILDREN'S BOOKS

WunderMillBooks.com